PARADE
OF STORMS

OTHER BOOKS BY EVELYN LAU

POETRY

You Are Not Who You Claim
Oedipal Dreams
In the House of Slaves
Treble
Living Under Plastic
A Grain of Rice
Tumour
Pineapple Express
Cactus Gardens

MEMOIR

Runaway: Diary of a Street Kid
Inside Out: Reflections on a Life So Far

NOVELS

Other Women

SHORT STORIES

Fresh Girls and Other Stories
Choose Me

PARADE OF STORMS

EVELYN LAU

ANVIL PRESS // VANCOUVER, CANADA

Library and Archives Canada Cataloguing in Publication

Title: Parade of storms / Evelyn Lau.
Names: Lau, Evelyn, 1971- author.
Identifiers: Canadiana 20250170264 | ISBN 9781772142457 (softcover)
Subjects: LCGFT: Poetry.
Classification: LCC PS8573.A7815 P37 2025 | DDC C811/.54—dc23

Cover design: Rayola.com
Interior layout: HeimatHouse
Author photo: John Patterson

Represented in Canada by Publishers Group Canada and Distributed by Raincoast Books, and in the United States from Asterism Books (Seattle).

The publisher gratefully acknowledges the financial assistance of the Canada Council for the Arts, the Canada Book Fund, and the Province of British Columbia through the B.C. Arts Council and the Book Publishing Tax Credit.

Anvil Press Publishers Inc.
P.O. Box 3008, Station Terminal
Vancouver, B.C. V6B 3X5 Canada
www.anvilpress.com

Printed and bound in Canada.

In memory of John Ehni, Steve Patterson,
Trudi Patterson and Larry Wong

CONTENTS

Part One: Atmospheric River

POST-SURGERY

Was this the end of indulgence? The days that followed
were stamped flat, leeched of pleasure —
a roster of duties, chores, lurching awake
in the night to fumble pills into his palm
to stave off infection, the roaring pain.
Spilled water from the cryo-cuff machine
blanched the hardwood, a slick of urine
glazed the plastic pail bedside. Crumbs on the patio,
pie crust and seeded toast, worried between his fingers,
for the birds. His pupils black dots pinned in blue —
you recall that summer from your youth,
Dilaudid sweetening your blood to syrup,
bite down on the yearning to set sail
again, towards that candied horizon.
Bite down on your own midlife complaints —
buzzing of nerves, twitching of tendons,
joints glowing cherry-red. In the high-acuity ward
he was a downed beast with a waxen face,
tethered with cords, wires, oxygen tubes,
punctured and stapled, slit open. It was Christmas
in the hospital, strung with dollar-store bulbs.
You shuffled along sidewalks slicked with ice
to visit him, past tent cities, addicts curled
over their tinfoil and lumps of coal —
figures flash-frozen into the strangest bonsai,
deformed by storm surge, king tide.
Pigeons hunkered down in the park,
tucked into their own bodily warmth, self-sufficient.

ATMOSPHERIC RIVER

After, you would join others at the beach,
greedy for a glimpse of wreckage —
barge slammed against seawall, containers
like a copper fort bricked against sky.
Scrawl of flip-flops, kelp lacing the bike path.
A fishing vessel propped against rocks, deck
at right angles to the shoreline, split open.

On TV, Merritt slept under a skim
of coffee-brown floodwater —
a city submerged, tops of trees and roofs
tickling the rippled surface. A month of rain
in two days, and farms in Abbotsford
morphed into private islands
on a vast inland lake, livestock paddling
through cranberry bogs. Zigzagged cars
strewn across the Coquihalla, a medley
of tree trunks and metal, mummified in mud.

During the storm you were on the bridge,
forcing your body against the wind like a mountaineer.
Savage sounds of banners snapping,
signs and awnings cracking, safety glass imploding.
Decades ago, you stood on this summit shredding
sheet after sheet of paper into the night ocean,
groping for courage to follow
their ghostly descent. Now you cling to life
like any stubborn old thing, clawing your way across —
headlights surging on one side,
swallowing sea on the other. The atmospheric river
breaching the banks of sky, swamping the horizon.

PARADE OF STORMS

In the calm between one atmospheric river
and the next, I paused on the bridge,
watched a man string Christmas lights across his balcony.
Distance blurred detail, so all that was visible
in the mysterious vapour were armloads of sparkle
he hauled as if from the sea, a vast net of glitter
he looped over and under the rails, over
and under, golden orbs and silver spheres
spilling forth from his embrace —

There in the blue mist, drowned boats
sinking to the creek bottom, the rains fell
and kept falling like punishment.
This is the end times, we'd all agreed —
saturated earth crumbling, dislodging hillsides,
houses. Blighted harvests, bare store shelves,
cargo trains tumbling into crevasses.
Would the pipelines explode? Doomsday activists
sat cross-legged at intersections,
horses stampeded through soaked farmland,
numb faces on the news listed a litany of losses —
homes, livelihoods, generations of labour.

I kept watching. He was like a fisher
from a fairy tale, soon to catch the magic flounder
in his humble net, the one that could grant wishes —

KINTSUGI

Here there was no end to what they would spend
on beauty. Planting, re-planting,
shrubs plucked and clipped into topiary,
floral dioramas tweaked weekly. Shop entrances
garlanded with creamy blooms, spilling
down pillars, banisters. Even the alleys
strung with parasols, hanging baskets
beset by bees. The sky painted
bonny blue, and yet —

dread seeps in from the edges,
pipes groaning through walls,
bubbles sagging with leaked water plinking
a line across the ceiling. Calculations
late into the night, how to sustain
the unsustainable — levies, taxes,
strata fees — while drywall
drinks the mildew. The new year's intention?
Just to stay on this side of the tracks,
where cherry blossoms mend the seams
of sidewalks, like gold repairing
what's been broken. Where a million-dollar
chandelier flashes under a bridge, spinning
like a leggy ballerina, skirts flared.
Yesterday you headed east, past the boundary —

tent cities, scorched parks, passers-by
blinking out of SRO burrows, pocked skins
flinching at the stings of sunlight. You trod
on sidewalks baked with excrement, slimed
with dumpster trash, spiked with needles.
Human figures prostrated themselves
in doorways, foreheads to filth, bare bums skyward —

THE PORCUPINE'S HEARTBEAT

He loved to quote Sun Tzu: *If you sit by the river long enough,*
you will see the body of your enemy float by.
What he didn't say: the bodies of loved ones, too.
Spring and it's death, death, death even as the rains

plump the peonies, as rosebushes spew
blooms onto the cobbled path. Sage and lilac
dust the air so that, tugging open the patio door,
I nearly choke. Recall the thickened water I fed you

spoonful by spoonful, a gelatinous broth
that slimed your mouth and dribbled
onto the daisy-patterned hospice gown. It snowed
in April, then. Boots and puffers came un-stuffed

from the backs of closets, grim-faced commuters
shivered their way onto transit. On TV, we watched
the San people in Namibia hunt for sustenance
by digging burrows into the earth, listening

for the porcupine's heartbeat, hauling
their appalling dinner home over their shoulders,
quills splayed in peacock glory. No,
we couldn't compare one person's pain

to another's. Hail drilled the hospice grounds
the day you slumped over, didn't have the strength
to lift the weight of your own head on its bent stalk.
One morning we drifted into sleep while looking

at each other, your thumb stroking a lifeline
into my palm, as rain gusted against the panes,
nurses strode from room to room. For weeks
this was the space we held, a glass house

in which each breath thrummed, throbbed,
swollen with impending stoppage.
Silver light drizzled in. Nobody told me:
when it's over, I would sacrifice an entire summer

just for one more day inside that bubble,
down the corridor of dying strangers, your nameplate
still fixed to the last door on the left.

ERASURE

At first there was a murmur in the air, like a swarm of crickets.
A gurgle in the pipes, patter of rain on the roof.
Upstairs, the tenant drew a bath, tugged on headphones,
stepped away singing. Foam surged to the porcelain lip

and tumbled over, a cascade of lavender sprigs,
blown roses. You put your ear to the wall,
heard a percussive drumming,
then the sky ripped open. Water gushed

from shower fixtures, streamed down
stained tiles. Moisture in the shapes of clouds
bloomed across the popcorn ceiling.
When the corners of your bedroom peeled apart,

you were waiting, buckets in both arms,
for the blessing. The flood lashed out
in ropes of silver — spat, coiled, flung
itself in too many directions to catch.

It licked the covers of books signed by authors
now dead, or so deep in dementia they didn't
know their own words. Sighing, water soaked
into boxes stored in the closet, guzzled by stacks

of paper and ink thirsty for the bliss of erasure.
You sat on the edge of your bed, watched
the freshwater lake inch across the carpet.
Then the tiredness, the aching arms

from the weight of another young woman's
carelessness. You wanted nothing more
than to lie down, let the waves lap
over your body, flood the shore.

OCEAN HOUSE/KAYSUUN VILLAGE

When you first arrived, you felt mutilated.
The ground itself repelled you, a green sponge
springing you off the surface of Haida Gwaii.
Black ooze of slug, sharpened stakes protruding
from trees, moss, nurse logs. You were nothing,

in the presence of nothing. What could heal you?
Waxstar, red alder, licorice root, chickweed,
stinging nettle. A Haida love song unspooling
in the drizzle, a girl with a drum and a braid
of hair. The blue bud of a spruce tip shocked

your mouth with herbal sweetness, bitter seed.
Everyone saw bald eagles, five persimmon
circles in the limestone cliff, felt the blurred
slouch of longhouses returned to earth,
except you. You couldn't detect the presence

of the ancient, plundered village, trace
the remnants of a retaining wall. You woke
in the floating lodge certain of footsteps, an intruder.
Across the inlet you glimpsed a landslide,
its path of erasure, remembered how he took everything

green and stable with him when he left.
Crouched on shore, you scratched symbols on rocks
with slivers of shale, skidded on sheets
of seaweed. Jellyfish gasped and billowed
in the cove — breathing in, out.

RESTORATION

After the flood, everything became porous.
Gardens of mould grew along baseboards,

beads of quivering liquid hung from the ceiling
like abacus strings. The air was jelly, and shivered.

Rot had seeped in, started to spread.
A bloom of licorice flowers blemished

the bone surface. Nothing you had done
to maintain the exterior mattered —

caulk brittle as dried fish skin,
haze between double-paned windows,

sills brimming with desiccated bees adrift
on rank rainwater. You sniffed it in your sleep,

a sour mildew reek like a heap of damp towels.
On the terrace below, a family of crows feasted

on the breast of a woodpecker they pecked
to death, its half-sobs waking you at dawn.

Anyone could come and chisel away
your floors and ceiling, carve holes in your walls

call it a mistake. Bundles of dust, splinters
razor blades left at your feet. Finally

you were close to something — epiphany? Collapse?
Arms flung open, bare-faced to the storm.

FRACTURE

First week of November, and already you're in bed
by noon. Tile-blue skies, tangerine trees —

yet here you lie, nursing the invisible fracture.
He said he was leaving and, three weeks later,

he was gone. *Say you miss me, admit it,*
you wrote into the appalled silence.

The humiliation of how you seized pleasure
from his slightest touch — was this where you began

to lose him? Mornings you "forest bathe"
in the urban park, past the highrise where a man

flew to the sidewalk, the gore he left behind
dispersed in a pile of fire-hose foam. Yes,

the North Koreans are starving and the migrant
caravan is crawling closer to the border and we are

sick of our good fortune. You've lived too long
in disorder, hoarding the remains —

this latest flood washed the bedroom contents
into the living room, where heaps of clothes

and soaked papers now form a kind of shoreline,
a ragged littoral border. A friend calls from California —

Come with us to Mexico, say yes —
but you turn away from the glare of chlorine,

bowl-shaped drinks flavoured like watermelon
and bubble gum. You say *thank you,* say *no*.

Read poems by lamplight in the 4 PM dark.
Consider what can't be redeemed, what's left.

MINDFUL

for Kurt Aydin

I was coming out of the long darkness
when a streetlight shone on the rain-slick hedge,

and — oh. Green gleam in the corner of my eye,
barbed holly, Chinese jade. Had I held my breath

all winter, blind to beauty? Tonight we contemplate
a dun sesame seed for the count of five —

breath in, out, in. The scarlet stones
that circle your wrist press cool

against the heated thrust of your blood —
a monk's simple beads, when all your life

you've lunged for more, bashing yourself
along the way. Let's say tonight, *this is enough* —

bronze glow in the west, fog slouching south,
bridge visible again. We'll sip priceless tea

from some forgotten village, seek notes
of sticky rice, apple pear, snow leopard —

strain it through our teeth like mud-water.
Pay attention to that first flush of saliva,

the aroma hoarded inside the upturned porcelain lid.
I was drowning in that darkness when all along,

here, this cloud of flowers.

Part Two: Heat Dome

HEAT DOME

for Lian Gies

The world we knew has burned away.
Still, something here remains —

sweat-stung, breathless under the heat dome,
we slosh into the ocean at Deep Bay,
cut-glass waves surging, garlands of seaweed
sweeping past like leis set adrift at a sea burial.

Your fingers comb the marine tangle, collagen beadwork
swollen with sap, grassy strands stippled
with bubble wrap. Let this belong to us
while wildfires incinerate northern towns,

wooden churches combust on reservations.
Swell of salt in my eyes and an eagle
cheeping on the highest branch of the cedar
in your garden of crispy Jennies. The ocean shifts

curdles in my circling arms —
tiny dead crabs like bone brooches,
splay of sea worm, blob of foam and stirred slime.
For so long I've been bleached of words,

sun-stunned, unfocussed, the air muddled
corrosive. Let us not turn away
when other figures brave the beach, picking their way
down rocky paths, finding the thread of sand

between sharp stones to the sea.

HOPE WILDFIRE

The first drop of water on earth is still here,
Steve says. *Everything recycles. When they cremate us —*
there'll be steam, right? So after we go, the first time
it rains, that'll be me, pissing on you.
We are laughing, because what can you do.
Because Trudi beams from her wheelchair:
Oh, we've had great lives. Last week on the drive

to Summerland we saw the harvest moon
perched on a hilltop, counted it as one of our
three good things that day
for maximum happiness. We had the best
of everything, we told ourselves —
bowls of forbidden rice on the restaurant patio,
views of sun-bleached cliffs, clear-cut subdivision
above terraced wineries. Spiderwebs draped
over groomed hedges, lavender crumbling
into a last flurry of purple scent. We drifted

from pleasure to pleasure, drenched in the lake's
darkening blue of late summer. Crickets hopped
along the gravel path, minnows flickered
in moss-tangled water. I floated face-down
in the waves off Rotary Beach where last weekend
the E. coli counts were off the charts. For once
we didn't turn on the evening news with its
humanitarian crises, its *millions displaced* —
rising floodwaters in Pakistan,
earthquakes in rural China, and what's
going on with that nuclear power plant in Ukraine?
Instead we spooned cherry custard ice cream
on the deck, swooned. It might have been perfect

but on that last day we woke
to a shrivelled red dime in the sky, a dense

atmosphere of smoke. We drove home through
the Hope wildfire, buckets swinging from helicopters
whirring in mist that wasn't mist, or damp fog,
but *the worst air quality in the world,* the radio said.
Mountainous terrain wreathed in flames,
rows of torched evergreens, cinders raining
onto the highway. We drove, windows up
sweating, tasting carcinogens.

CARBON

Now the province blackens with wildfires,
embers flicked across the lake by wind gusts,
sparks like cigarette ends torching the tea-stained
cliffs. Forever homes on the hilltop, sprawled
across acreage, temporary after all. What malfunction
in me wants it all to burn? I never worked enough hours
to love or list, sell or renovate, though lust ignited me
at the sight of design porn. Marble backsplashes,
statement lighting, claw-foot tubs —
up in smoke. European appliances,
memory foam mattresses, luxury plank
flooring — *poof*. Yesterday the apartment keys
slipped from my fingers, trembled at the lip
of the gap, plunged down the elevator shaft.
For a few hours, nothing belonged to me.
I roamed the city nameless, empty-handed,
searching for water to sluice the grit of cinders
off my tongue. The taps at the community centre
were rusted, dry. Above, the sun a wrinkled red plum
tucked into a bowl of ashes, covered in muslin.

SUMMER BREAK

with a closing line by Rainer Maria Rilke

These sapped days of summer, swollen with indolence —
you've shrugged off that extra layer
of meaning, the poems that knit a skin
between you and the flayed world. Words, words —
why add to the clutter, when self-help books say
to take your life down to the studs, as if your life
were a room to be emptied, gutted? Both the physical
and digital worlds stacked to the ceiling, the cloud,
with words, and look where it got us.
Maybe this is the wisdom of surrender, or more
likely the lure of easy pleasures —
Taco Tuesdays, backyard barbecues,
weekend jaunts to the timeshare. Months
without precipitation, and the air puckers
with the perfume of back alley dumpsters.
Screens flicker with forest fires roaring
through the mountains, bruise-coloured banks
of smoke, flashes of flame. In Europe, in America,
tourists limp past fountains and statues,
fanning themselves, haloed by haze, humidity.
If they stumbled on the sidewalks, their braced palms
would fuse to bubbling concrete. But we do our part —
separate plastics from glass, organics
from landfill, in our small-footprint condos.
When the fire alarm gongs at midnight, we trudge
down the stairwell in slippers, the outer air
lukewarm, sludgy. Firefighters muscle past the gates,
slung with hoses, and the realization clobbers you
like a crow digging its claws into your scalp —
all summer you've written nothing, there is nothing
that makes you worth saving. Neighbours yawn
in the ashen half-dark, eyes down, texting.
A flashlight beam scissors back and forth
a shuttered suite. *Who, if I cried out,*
would hear me among the angels' hierarchies?

FIT, FABULOUS, 50

The operating room glare of 3 a.m.

*

That sense of something *not quite right* —
tilted, askew. A fog in the brain —
mornings groping through mist flickering
with cinders, carcinogens.
A sinkhole that yawns open in the day.

*

Focus shifts, shudders and blurs,
like the clanking of phoropter lenses
at the optometrist's, letters taking a split-second
to swim into proper position.
Black squiggles in sight-lines.

*

Fibroids deform the uterus.
Spotless for months, then a burst of blood
almost aortic in volume and velocity,
drenching tampons, pads, panties.
Towels sop up the crime scene,
patterns of spatter.

*

Body temp set to simmer.
Dry-eyed weeping, lashing rage
followed by flashes of extreme joy —
gratitude for the blooming cactus,
crumpled linens, mouth-feel of chocolate.

*

Paused, we shed hair like skin cells,
carpet the hardwood with fur.
Leave forensic evidence to say we were there.

MAiD

for Steve and Trudi Patterson

When the hour arrived, I lowered the blinds
on the fractured night, lit all the candles in the room —

There was the housewarming candle, dropped
on my doorstep a quarter century ago,
still fragrant with green tea,
trussed in crumbled gauze ribbon —

The Chinese lantern, peacock brocade,
slubbed silk, torqued iron. A splurge
from a boutique in Chinatown, long shuttered —

Two Himalayan salt pillars, salvaged
from a corner of the garbage room,
a neighbour's discards. Rough-hewn,
slabs of ice veined with terracotta —

A row of dollar-store votives,
winking out in minutes —

A row of beeswax votives, handcrafted,
honey-dipped, gifted by a colleague who
cared about *local, organic, clean burning*.
Possibly edible, in an emergency —

A silver tin poured with wax, bestowed
by a student at end of term, artisan-signed,
numbered, infused with *crisp, floral notes of*
bergamot, lavender, violet —

A stone holder, nested in your brother's palm
our first Xmas together. Imperfect,
perfect, mottled with the porosity
asymmetry of a rock on the beach,
battered by salt, storm —

I didn't know what else to do. How to mark
or mourn your lives at this hour, how to carry
the knowledge that at any moment
your breaths would falter, stop —

I sat, alone for the first time
in decades. A bower of flames bloomed,
heating the room. Wicks snapped,
sank into ponds of liquid wax —
twists of carbon smoked the air.

Goodbye, I said to Steve and Trudi,
miles away at the clinic. Waved my hand
through the forest of dimming candles, called out
goodbye, goodbye —

Part Three: Dull Emergency

DULL EMERGENCY

What's up with these open-ended days?
Under-employed, we shuffle to the beach,
stoop for shells as if for souvenirs from afar —
Sanibel Island, maybe, where once we stuffed
our luggage with shells the size of fists.
Now we point overhead and grunt like cavemen,
agog at the novelty of a plane searing the sky
as if it were the first flight out of here.
Stranded, a year into the pandemic,
no one has any news to share, vocabularies
reduced to *virus, vaccine, variants* —
that dull emergency of the daily count.
Time stretches, sags, goes pear-shaped.
There's little to say but still we mumble
behind our masks, eyes widening or squinting
in exaggerated empathy or sorrow, desperate
to communicate. A straggling sun
casts dips and hollows in the sand,
washes the shore in weak light. Campers crowd
the parking lot, snowbirds shivering in portable saunas,
pop-up tents in this *California of Canada*.
But we're lucky, so lucky. Driftwood in strange,
soft-serve shapes, algae-green water. Given
another chance, we'll snorkel with mantas at midnight,
paraglide from cliff-faces, jounce on camels
across blinding deserts. We'll squeeze
into seats on prop planes, knees to chins, and scream
with joy at the adventure. All those words
we held back? Next time. Just you wait.

ODE TO CODEINE

When the borders close, it becomes your ticket to travel,
your virus passport, your immunity. It returns
the colours to you, the textures —

glaze of canary sun, rattle of palm fronds.
Heat haloes blurred around vehicles, passersby.
It returns the surfers, bobbing like plastic toys
in the surf. Texas donuts the size of your head,
boardwalk air deep-fried in saturated fat
clinging to your clothes for days.
Toothless women selling churros from Styrofoam coolers,
blank-eyed kids grouped on motel stoops,
towels tacked over windows. You glimpse
again the lights of Santa Monica at night, rides careening,
metal shrieking, pinwheel of the Ferris wheel ablaze.
Once you were so high you tripped,
shredded your knee on Ocean Boulevard,
the blood oozing down your leg as pleasing
as raspberry coulis drizzled on a dessert plate.
Once you were a speck in the human tide
that surged down to the shore, ultraviolet
bleaching the landscape flat, shellacked —

Now it wraps you in cling film, renders you weightless.
You drift, the days a string of hard candy
melted down to cough syrup —
on vacation, inoculated against everything.

LOST LAKE

for Janie Chang

Then came another stretch of silence, the longest.

Your mind stopped its casting and bobbing.
The glass waters went opaque, churned with rock flour.
What was burbling below? No fish in the leaping river
but someone's spray-painted them onto boulders,
lavender and jade salmon struggling against currents
of glitter. You were *on holiday*, had been for longer

than anyone knew. You trudged down forest trails,
inhaling moss and fungus, rotting stumps,
scanning for bears. Found claw marks
raked into a trunk, oozing wounds in bark.
Pines sketched with frost, maples charred black.
The sky, closed over. You weren't sure of anything,

except that some zenith had been passed
and now you were on the declining slope,
loose pebbles skittering. A sense of drift.
Maybe the mind was erasing itself, that final mercy
of age. Windows onto a brick wall. A view
around the bend — metal shed, sliver of ski hill.

Lake after lake glimpsed through greenery,
yet no through road you could see.

WASTE

The Lord God is always with us, the chaplain says
out of nowhere, spoiling an otherwise normal conversation —
climate change, cost of living, war in Ukraine.
Turns to you, or what's left of you —
stick figure bundled in blankets,
eyes twin stitches in a sallow face,
gaping cave of mouth. *Are you at peace, John?*
We wait in strained silence, for what doesn't come —
a confession? Words of wisdom?
The urge to mock rises in me
like roiling water, a desire to desecrate
anything that hints at the holy.
Leaning over you, my hair soaks up your smell —
waxy limbs, dry scurf, a honeyed rot
that blooms in gusts between cracked lips.
The hospice air is a cloud of bacteria
sprayed with sanitizer, a miasma of skin flakes,
diaper stench that coats me in the stink
of the grave. Never mind the spells of grace
in this room, hovering of nurses and volunteers,
choreography of movements scripted to your needs —
my hand dipping spoons into pureed soup,
your nephew bending straws into ice water.
Maybe we've spent too many hours
encouraging the light, prattling with fake cheer,
drawing your dying gaze to the camellia bush
outside the window, sparrows at the bird feeder.
Maybe there's only this body, and what's left:
scaffolding of ribs, stumps of carbon teeth,
the rapt look on your face
as waste burbles forth from between your legs
in a low rumble beneath the covers.

HOSPITAL

1.

Murmurs behind masked faces, prods and probes,
pain that ricocheted in zigs and zags,
a clamour that couldn't be calmed.
Literally seeing stars — lightning, too.
I wanted to vamoose, but it seemed body
and soul were joined after all, their connection
tenuous but true. The masks kept asking
if I was *all right*, with each incursion of needle
and drill, finger and microscope. Sometimes their eyes
went soft, sagging at the corners with empathy,
and I worried for these young doctors —
they were like hermit crabs quivering
in the open, seeking shelter. A hard carapace.
The one who flushed tomato-red around his mask,
apologized for "man-handling" me —

2.

Suspect smells in the clinical air, a sugary whiff
of cotton candy or crème brûlée
masking the reek of infection, decay.
The burning of bone. Those weeks were a blur
of waiting rooms, pills shaken into my palm,
wasted days of September sunshine.
An impenetrable skin between the sick
and healthy, like the plastic dome around
the boy in the bubble all those decades ago:
fuzzed image on TV in the wooden cabinet
at one end of the orange living room,
us crouched at the other end, straining
to see, nervous of its cancerous rays —

3.

Most people ended up here sooner
or later — olive chairs in beige corridors,
drained grey faces in limbo. A fermata, a staycation.
Work deadlines could wait, put on pause,
while the emergency took over. Another cymbal-crash
of pain, its slow seeping subsidence.
I remembered how to leave my body,
floated pleasantly around the ceiling for a while.
Touched down when I transferred thousands
of dollars from my account to the specialist's —

4.

Pain clamped down, breath-stealing. I swatted
at the fireflies pestering my vision —
mosquitoes, horseflies. Thought of my GP,
his lineless hands pressing my stomach,
the distracting closeness of his young male body
radiant with health. Diagnosed last year with Stage 4 cancer
at 36. I watched the video he made, how he blinked
and began, "Dear friends..." as if he were a child
who believed all strangers to be benevolent —
as if they had never been harmed,
never caused harm.

5.

Learn to leave your body, I wanted to say to him. As
fine a piece of advice as any. *Then return.*

SIX OF ONE, HALF A DOZEN OF THE OTHER

We had front-row seats to the spectacle —
a would-be jumper! —
from the Free Weights window at the gym. Every so often,
members would sidle over from Cardio

or Personal Training to check on her progress.
"Still there?" Yes, braced outside her balcony railing
in the condo across the lane. Hugging the rails,
sometimes she would lean forward

or stretch out a leg — a cramp? —
or a foot, as if dabbling it in water, testing
the temperature. Silent from where we watched,
though she must have muttered or shouted

at the commotion below, the excess of cop cars,
ambulances and fire trucks blocking the street,
bystanders angling phones skyward.
Her hair was dun, she wore a pilled fleece that hung

on her gaunt frame, she wasn't young.
Her balcony, a kaleidoscope of colour —
potted plants, wind chimes, glittery streamers —
now seemed a desperate hedge against despair.

Red and blue lights rotated beneath her
in the smoky August air, ash from nearby
forest fires greying the atmosphere.
She opened her mouth — was she yawning?!

Thrust out that foot again, ankle lazily tracing
circles in one direction, the other.

DEMENTED

My neighbour roams the corridors
like an unwanted child or grey-haired ghost,
wearing cat PJs, dollar-store slippers
with paper soles, housecoat laced with holes
at the cuffs and collar. Tacks notes printed
in serial-killer all-caps on the bulletin board,
scratches hieroglyphs into the stainless steel
elevator doors. Some days panic scrawls
her features, she doesn't know the day
or month or what human action
is required of her —

fobs in and out of the lounge
in senseless rounds, fumbles
light switches on, off. Follows me
down the street at a shuffling distance,
bed-head askew, backpack over her shoulders,
corners me in the corner store:
Just wanted to say hi to my favourite
neighbour in the whole wide world!
Phones four times a day because the hot water

is *too* hot, *burning* hot, she's worried
someone in the building will scald themselves —
then a fifth call: *Please check your hot water,*
it's not even lukewarm. We'll be having cold
showers tomorrow! This is a decade after
her mother was diagnosed with dementia,

would stare at her daughter during care home
visits and hiss, *You have the ugliest eyes*
I've ever seen. She bawled telling me this,
hands shaking, by the mailboxes in the lobby
while I tutted in sympathy, edged away.
What is our "duty of care," one human

to another? Now I screen all calls,
gesture at the foam plugs in my ears
when she sidles by, shut the door
in her perplexed face. Then the whisper
from the other side, hurt, sly:
But I just wanted to say how lovely
you look today. Don't worry,
I won't bother you anymore.

Part Four: Cursing, Flailing

CURSING, FLAILING

1.

The world is on the brink of nuclear war,
says a voice on the radio, near the border
between Oregon and California. Our first road trip
post-pandemic, and motel rooms groan with cold
even as plum blossoms line the freeway. In America
food mashes into sweet pablum
against the roofs of our mouths —

2.

a stir of chemicals and enriched flour, pre-digested.
Ding-Dongs shaped like hockey pucks, corn chips
pushed through an extruder. 99 cents for a cup
of soda swill, small or X-large, so I cradle
a bucket-sized container of pop in my lap,
docile as a doped baby. Thanks to COVID
every plastic item comes wrapped in an extra film

3.

of plastic, and turd-coloured rooms reek
of hospital-grade disinfectant. Praise to plastic straws
instead of paper tubes that disintegrate
in carbonation, leaving mush to slurp up!
Praise to the gleam of plastic cutlery,
its utility and malleability, its future journey adrift
for decades through miraculous oceans!
We unwrap burgers the size of our heads

4.

while parked beside a tent city, gnaw gritty patties,
lick sauce dispensed in measured dollops.
On a beach between San Francisco and Santa Cruz
I crawl into a lean-to built by a homeless man
who will reclaim it at sunset. Will bombs

find us here? Only the ocean's painful roar, the sound
of a million creatures dying. It seems a crime

5.

to walk in America, the few pedestrians
stumbling out of trailer parks and bars
scanning for trouble and cursing, flailing.
The motel lobby sign says there's a $100. fine
for using hair dye — it ruins the towels —
but *everyone*, the clerk says, *wants to change*
their identity. Young women pass me in the halls,
hoodies up, PJ bottoms flapping, slippers slapping.
I squat on a curb by the entrance — COVID stacked away
the lobby chairs — and guests ask, *Ma'am, do you work here?*

N'AWLINS

Festooned with beads, dusted in *beignet* sugar,
baubles clank against our soft stomachs
as we trip down filthy streets
reeking of lust, pools of urine steaming

beneath bricked and shuttered shotguns. Masked figures
rear like horse heads against a wrought-iron
sky. Is this the America he promised us?
Now that he's gone, his ghost roams restless —

unappeased by altars in voodoo shops, spells dissolved
in a glass of water under the bed, snags of Spanish moss
and alligator claws. Kratom in my purse and codeine
fizzing my blood, we gag at the shoeless scruff

who parades Bourbon St. with his cardboard sign:
Will lick pussy for anything. In the Lower Ninth Ward,
lots overgrown with weeds and grass form
a kind of parkland, slabs of foundation visible

like cemetery stones. Did you know a football field
of wetlands succumbs to saltwater every hour? On the cover
of *USA Today*, it's the farm states now where the levees
are gone. The couple from Huntsville says you just

keep moving on, rebuild in the wake of tornados,
hurricanes, floods. *What else y'all gonna do?*
Prepare to live in a motel by the freeway, food-shop
at gas station marts, camp under the overpass

littered with chopsticks, tampons, tire skins.
Still the trees are blue-black with grackles,
sunset a peach haze behind the water tower,
oil refinery. We are walking where maybe no one
has walked before.

SANS SOUCI

A bouquet of parrotfish gathered near the outcropping,
mouths fretting the aerated reef, bloated shapes
in silted water. They brushed past you like bladders,
cumulus in the water and a sieve of sand,
yet you stayed out there for hours, face-down —

inspecting a meaty clump of octopus,
spines of sea urchin blazed from rock crevices,
seaweed lofted like tumbleweed along the ocean floor.
This was the other world, a vast living room
with shades semi-drawn, scattershot drum

of rain pimpling the skin of the Pacific. Already
there's grit in your molars, whorls of your ears,
nail beds, nostrils, corners of salted lips and eyes —
already your body was crusted, a bearded shell.
Still you stayed until the water boomed

with sunlight, a bleached green cathedral.
Strange gnawing sounds scraped the silence —
parrotfish gnashing the coral for polyps,
a rude munching that delighted you
into gurgling laughter. You swallowed seawater,

spat lava sand, slurped oxygen until
your stomach cramped with effort, burned.
A school of coronetfish slicked past,
palm fronds lashing like eels. Then a wave
bashed you ashore, slashed by coral along the way.

LOWCOUNTRY

My wound is geography. It is also my anchorage, my port of call. — Pat Conroy

What music did he hear on this beach?
Thrum of sweetgrass, wing-beat of gulf fritillaries,
swerve/plash of dolphins, pelicans. Low moan

through magnolias in the cemetery. I tried to listen
but the island seemed opaque, unknowable —
mansion after mansion shuttered and silent,

scumbled staircases curved in ghostly embrace.
The bridge cracked open, its expanse white
as ibis. Reverb of a pile-driver in town,

pummelling another foundation.
Halfway down the pier, you found a fish
someone had hooked then flung

onto the wooden slats —
tail twitching, eyes rotating, its body
ridged and spiked, glazed in mud and weeds.

Mouth gasping in the caustic air.
While we watched, it blinked,
shuddered. Maybe I never understood

another creature's pain, blinded for decades
by my own. You tried to save it, though —
cradled it back to its own geography.

TARMAC

This evening on the six o'clock news,
Afghans swarmed the Kabul airport,
a stampede of hundreds in a swirl
of turbans and tunics — saffron, rosewater, pistachio —
rushing the tarmac, sprinting alongside
the US military jet as its crew taxied for takeoff.
Were they shouting, or huffing in fear, or just
running in awful, silent concentration, leaping
into the wheel well, onto slippery wings,
retracting staircase, railings,
grasping for a hand- or foothold anywhere
on that slick silver body? Figures clung
to the plane as it lifted into the sky, and then —

"We chose to pause the video here," the newscaster said.

Before they fell, dots plunging to the ground.
For one ecstatic moment they were pasted
in the blue and shining air, far above
the Taliban's hoisted flags, flying to America.

COMFORT INN

Sunset beyond the bristle of palm trees —
pomelo sky, nectarine sky,
then the side streets plunged into pitch.
Jacarandas, trash bins, rock gardens blurred
to granular black-and-white. He came from this dark,

slid himself next to me, soft-footed,
eyes not quite right, to breathe *hello* —
a spectre conjured from an admonition
not to walk alone at night, in a strange city,
in America. *Hi*, I replied,

passing polite, quickening my step.
Towards the hotel, its algae-green glow
under construction, tattered plastic shroud
swishing in the wind like strands of seaweed.
Crossed the lobby, summoned the elevator,

sensed a presence, hairs quivering.
Too late, he was there beside me,
slipping through the scraped and battered doors.
Your floor, he said when I enquired the floor,
and we were alone in that metal box,

some mysterious hydraulic system of cables
and pulleys transporting us
through the core of the building.
I'm with you, he said —
and later when I tell a friend she yelps,

At that point I would have pissed my pants!
So why wasn't I afraid?
He was less than half my age, prepared
to barter with his body, or plunder by force,
the way I'd been at that age, a wild creature

seeking some kind of shelter. Predator, prey:
only two types of people in the world, then.
In that tight elevator we breathed
the same dust-clogged air, like cellmates.
I'm with you. The half-drowned look

in his eyes, the ferret face. *Let me come with you.*
A stillness descended, time and motion
suspended in the lift, both of us
meditating on the coming violence —
No, I said then. Laughed a little, maybe.

No, but have a good night —
pressed Ground for him to go back down
as the doors whirred open. The air crackled,
sparked, the atmosphere shifted, settled.
Did he know? He let me go —

drifted back to the lobby, into
the Los Angeles night, alive at last sight.

Part Five: The Good Life

HOUSE & GARDEN

On the cover, you are washed in light —
clad in pale linens, barefoot, "at home."
Beyond the gleaming deck, surge of sand, beach grass.
The Pacific a glazed fever dream, burned blue.
Turquoise pool suspended over tiered garden,
jewelled wife, laughter in your eyes —
This is winning. Sure, it is, and a sour wave
crests my throat, the citric sting of envy —
scrolling through evidence of your life
in magazines, all Dom Perignon
and Wagyu tenderloin, the famed
architect's house you call home.

Three decades ago you whispered,
I want to run away with you —
and now you wear the look of a man
ecstatic at escaping the worst mistake of his life.
What luck! It made you expansive, philanthropic.
A tithe to the gods: your name in script
on theatres, hospitals, public spaces.

Once we grappled in dim rooms, bruised
each other through a haze of mini-bar vodka.
Scent of cut limes, sea spray, the taste of blood.
Leave my mind, I begged for years after.
Son of an immigrant street sweeper, now
you would carve into slabs of gold if you could,
guzzle goblets of liquid gold. Every room
of your house overlooks the sea, but one —
it overlooks a garden of rare palm trees,
a centuries-old statue of Buddha.
All of it, yours. I remember the cold bones
of your face turned away, lust, refusal.
My small, simmering life wavering, then
going on and on without you.

THE GOOD LIFE

His new wife's face isn't visible
in the press photo, just the tilt of her head
like a drowsing tulip, a lock of hair curlicued
over one shoulder. The shape of her body
a spit-polished violin, arms and throat
hidden — revealed in slivers, slashes —
black silk stretching over a pale hip, thigh.
From the pleat at the corner of one eye,
you can see, she's laughing.

He stands legs apart, bespoke tux straining
to disguise a body broadened over the years,
coarsened. Gone those sculpted features,
buried beneath sugary layers of indulgence,
the good life. Mouth gaped in laughter, he's almost
guffawing, cat that swallowed the canary.
A background of soaring marble, scarlet carpet,
that storied glamour. You recall his touch,
how he handled objects with such care,

reverence almost, the simplest things —
porcelain neck of a sake bottle, bills for the valet,
your fingers meshed in his. Until he didn't.
The dusky black fingerprints he inked
onto your breasts, how you ached to display
this forensic evidence of his interest, to prove
a man like him wanted someone like you.
What had he said once, over drinks
at the Four Seasons? *You would be fascinating,*
even if you were just the maid here.
It sounded like a compliment, but maybe he equated you
with grime, servitude, and that throb of excitement
in his belly was the sort that pulses at the prospect
of touching something unclean, possibly contagious.
It didn't matter. In that moment he wanted you,
he said so. You beamed like a child, believing
you were good enough, and his life could be yours.

RAVENOUS

Soon your life's work will be signed off
into silence, the north tower bulldozed into rubble —
small wonder this grief inside you
has cracked into a chasm, that you are scrabbling
in the debris. But here at La Pentola,
glass spheres toss the grey light
back and forth, the summer mizzle.
Spark and fizz of prosecco, silver and linen,
pucker of warm olives on our tongues.
Here is our musical interlude, our fermata —

far from the blackout room where you crouched
all week, shouting mantras into the silence.
But even in the fall, the blessing.
A girl has come into your life, *so beautiful*
you say, flicking the Samsung screen,
but she isn't really. Just young. There's always
a girl and you are always lurching hand over hand
to that shuddering height, nerves sparking, craning out
for the burst of a kiss. A kind of ecstasy —

suspense, withholding. And now we're ravenous
as beasts at a salt lick, sucking and tonguing
the sharp pits, dragging crusts through an oil slick,
crunching through clams seeded with sand.
I've watched you eat an entire crab, tear apart
its steaming carcass, capped teeth clamping down —
tugging, extracting. The sweetness.

CREATURE

When he says he's leaving, his face
is caged in light. Later you circle back
to this moment, this joy that haloes his features.
Like the friend he mistakes you for,
you contort your own face to mirror
his pleasure, to share in his good fortune —
you distort your features
until you feel deformed. He would flinch
if you cried on his shoulder, if you gasped,
gulped back tears like a girl. He expects
better, after all he's taught you —
how to squish a spider without shuddering,
how to saunter past a person in need,
how to shut down. Perhaps
he's even a little proud of his protégée,
the way you greet this news with bright
dry eyes. If there's one thing that makes
him squeamish, it's tears, but that's not
the purge your body desires.
You're closer to vomiting on his shirt
than dampening it with sobs.
He's re-arranged you, reached in
and re-shaped you, and now he's leaving
you. Nausea squeezes your stomach
and curdles, a bacteria liquefying
your insides, so that you need the toilet
more than a tissue. He doesn't see
any of this, teeth bared in a smile —
a creature crouched to spring, gut you alive.

WRITE AN EKPHRASTIC POEM, SHE SAID

Field of wheat, sky with cartoon clouds.
This painting is Edenic, pours forth light
like a portal, but what he loves is what you would erase —
two shirtless men in the foreground,
one hunting down the other with his lust.
The ripple of their muscles, going against the grain.
You wish for emptiness — as if you were some sage!
No, you are the woman longing for the man
who lurks in the grass, his gaze tugged
towards another man as if towards the sunrise.

You will never be able to deform yourself to spark that surge.
Slick lips, magenta trench, heels —
he would admire you without that thump of wanting.
The day you confessed your desire, he laughed,
covered his crotch like a diner placing
a palm over his wineglass, as if to say, *No, thank you.*

In this painting, one man parts the swaying wheat
to reach the other, their need a sudden lurch
into sensation, a quick gulp satisfied —
chaff in their hair, scratches on furred arms.
There, it's done. They go off in opposite directions,
sated, bored. Meanwhile he writes you again:
My friend, I'm thinking of you.

No, he says, *what you do isn't work.*
You have no idea what real work is.

Maybe you've grown used to the daze
of middle age, when the act of bending down
feels like forced labour. Never mind the work of rustling up
some feeble words of praise for this passing world.
You prefer to idle in the hammock of summer,
opposite float homes with their yellow Adirondacks,
marine traffic crisscrossing the creek.
In silence, notebook empty.
Are you kidding me? he says. *You live in a bubble,*

this isn't the real world. Here, the sky blushes
the colour of a peach Bellini, and teacup dogs peek
from handbags. It's that sort of neighbourhood —
every surface with a sheen to it, like coinage.
Yet it costs nothing to watch the back and forth of productivity —
swinging metal cranes, brisk freighters —
while a heron dives into the sewage-treated water,
a seagull wrestles a clamshell for its wriggling salty meat.
You worked for this, these hours
of contemplation, these soft years.

But it can all be taken away, he says, *at any moment.*
Already there's a fine grit in the air, smell of shit
staining the artificial grass borders.
That's why you avoid the news with religious fervour,
gaze out the window at burnt greenery
while light pours onto the bleached oak floors
like the aftermath of disaster. What kind of work
is this, to pay attention to the lesser things?
Who said it was a blessing? Nine-to-five exchanged
for a handful of words on a page —
more white space than words — for mornings

squinting at a screen, afternoons daydreaming
while the world groans in its endless labour.
Nights flailing in the inland sea. Nothing was left
to you, nothing given, and yet —

SINGULARITY

Scrambling onto rocks, this cumbersome clamber
in search of semi-solitude, border smudged
between water and sky. Airplanes monstrous overhead,
bloated contraptions from another century. In this one,
flâneurs beep and buzz in singularity.
Jet-skis swerve past, live-aboards
spit their sewage into the creek.
The shimmer of spawning herring —
dots and dashes milling the warped pilings.

Maybe this is your job for now, to idle
in the glare like a lizard, flicking your tongue
at words. The mottled surfaces of these rocks
veined and spattered, irradiated. You vow to stay
inside this moment, senses torched —
bright beetles, pampas grass, the holly berry
oozing. Black-and-white retinal blaze
of sun, rushing cloud, the rains.

HEECH (NOTHING)

after viewing Parviz Tanavoli's *Poets, Locks, Cages*
exhibit at Vancouver Art Gallery, 2023

Words have warped us. Even in praise,
in solidarity, the poet figures are deformed —

shaped like pitchforks, corroded barrels,
kitchen implements without the utility.

Blank, or mutilated — faces staved in.
My life's work has perverted me.

The blood the nurse draws from my arm,
spiralling through the tube, is diseased,

a seesaw of levels that indicate the body
has turned on itself. No one willing to receive

its gift of rage, so it tunnelled back inside.
Years ago I too thought there was a beloved,

but it was only a shape in the clouds,
a stream of birds, the rustle of water. Nothing

to heave yourself off a mountaintop for, Farhad.
This work that was meant to make us *freest*

of all mankind, instead curdled us,
impoverished us, peering green-eyed

at the capitalist world, its rites of buying
and selling — while we squeezed lemons,

while our faucets ran dry. Our hearts protected
by grillwork, scavenged from dump sites.

CAMPUS

It breaks with the force of a migraine,
this craving for *one more chance* —
now that it's too late, twin grooves
parenthesizing my mouth in the mirror
most mornings. Where was the sixteen-year-old
whose future this might have been —

plush campus quad, torched maples?
Squirrels halting mid-scamper across
brick walkways, acorns coddled in paws.
The students tasked with their own to-and-fro,
slung with backpacks like previous generations,

distraction in their eyes, flashes of delight.
Phones welded to palms, the world sized to fit
on screens, shrunken, made bearable —
historic floods, earthquakes, wildfires
rushing and tumbling and blazing
in their hands. Wrenched out of worry

to recall their manners, to reach out,
hold a door open, gesture directions,
suppressing winces of irritation
at the interruption. Honey and acid
in the air, cider of late-September light.

Would a degree have bought me ease?
A softer life? Hovering outside Arts,
here this time to beg employment,
not admission, again I feel *all wrong* —
awkward as an adolescent, marked
for failure. It's the same day, just later.

SENSORY DETAILS

> *It isn't true* that we don't remember... Every time we are triggered — which is to say, caught up suddenly in an unwanted, puzzlingly overwrought emotional reaction — that is the past showing up.
>
> — Gabor Maté with Daniel Maté,
> *The Myth of Normal*

It's true, you never forgot. When a student submits
a poem on turning tricks when she was a teen —
price of a hitched ride, a meal, a place to crash —
you remember. God help you, you even use the word
"trigger" in your feedback, like some snowflake.
Like someone whose skin is so sensitive it turns
against itself, blooms with rashes that itch and blister,
nerve pathways spiked like barbed wire. No!
You order the student to *exploit the sensory details,*
insist we need to *feel* the stranger's body —
elephantine wrinkling of his thighs, secret
cottage cheese whiff of his crotch. You urge her
to ransack her own body's map of memory,
its loci of pain, what those years on the street knit
into her crooked spine, clenched jaw,
how those nights by the side of the road
disfigured her. Instructing her, you can almost taste
that first trick, his sour gush swamping your throat...

The squeak of the truck's vinyl upholstery.
Sweet pine reek of the dangling air freshener.
The pushed-in lighter that could be used as a weapon —
you could have stamped a charred circle in his cheek,
screamed *no,* staggered towards the refinery
on the docks, the sea of tar and salt. *Weak, coward.*
The light in the cabin clicked on. He wanted
to see you, because you were fourteen —
he wanted to watch himself instructing you.

YEAR OF THE RABBIT

It was our last visit, our last meal
together, the last weekend of your life.
Not a restaurant I'd have chosen —
bright-lit, jammed with families,

wedged into a strip mall in Richmond.
Windows spackled with grease-stained menus,
fabric flowers, strings of red envelopes
and gold tassels to ring in the Lunar Year.

Our table in the midst of the commotion —
slurping of soups, a shrieking child,
clatter and chatter of dozens of diners.
We ordered chicken chow mein,

spicy eggplant with ground pork —
when the dishes arrived, the waitress
almost upended the tray into your lap.
Ay-ya! she exclaimed, clutching her chest

in horror, relief. An accident averted,
and we smiled in solidarity. There was
this pressure in my throat, this urge
to find the right words, but everything

about this place said it wasn't the time,
though there wouldn't be another. You wore
a brilliant white shirt, which made me wonder
what you would wear to your scheduled death —

then I couldn't think of anything else.
What makes up a life? You were telling me
about feasting on back-to-back episodes
of *Blue Bloods* while I kept mining my thoughts

for something meaningful to say, but there was only
the day-to-day. You plucked a wedge of onion
with your chopsticks, chewed, sighed
in satisfaction. I looked at your pale,

heavy hands — hands that had built decks,
laid foundations for houses,
wrangled children, grandchildren,
saved strangers. These hands with all

their mechanical knowledge and intimate
memory would be stilled on Monday.
Outside, in the parking lot drizzle,
shoppers wheeling grocery carts past us,

we said our goodbyes. My hand kept rising
to press your chest, I couldn't help it,
it was the only part of me that tried to say, *Stay*.

SUNSPOT

We drove through a snowstorm
of cottonwood to arrive at this sun spot —
place of small bickering, pent silences.
Peaches, cherries. I cradled a western painted turtle
between my palms, its rock shell hiding the glory
of striped and scrabbling legs, craning neck,
swooping totem designs on its plastron.

*

Seven white goats lit the cliff-face like torches.

*

We watched light shift over pale gold vineyards,
clouds stipple the surface of the lake, the earth.
You snorted when I strapped the snorkel mask
over my face — *There's nothing in this lake* —
nothing but honeycomb patterns of sun
in cool green water, strands of oxygen bubbling
through mire. I crept along the sandy bottom
in a landscape of pebbles and dunes, stumbling
like any explorer, rapt, soundless.

*

In abundance you could read only boredom, torpor.

*

Of course there were afternoons
I woke at the bottom of the lake, blinking
through a forest of undergrowth, unable to swallow
or struggle to the surface. It was always
underfoot, the tangled water —
awash in parking lots, seeping under lawns.
In Summerland, breathing was like drowning —
the air choked with lilacs, roses.

*

But there was the woman who passed us
on the boardwalk, beaming face turned to her companion —
The joy, she said, *oh, the joy!*

ACKNOWLEDGEMENTS

Several of these poems first appeared, in slightly different form, in *Geist*, *The New Quarterly*, *Ricepaper* and *Vallum*.

"Atmospheric River" was shortlisted for the City Poems contest, and geo-cached in a poetry app by CEDaR (UBC). "Mindful" was chosen for *Best Canadian Poetry 2025*, ed. Aislinn Hunter.

"Write an Ekphrastic Poem, She Said" and "*heech* (nothing)" are for Fiona Tinwei Lam. "Summer Break" is for Kevin Spenst.

Gratitude to the Canada Council and BC Arts Council, for time to write. The writer-in-residence program at Langara College, for providing such a welcoming, supportive environment that I almost refused to leave. The team at Anvil Press, for their warmth, dedication and flashes of brilliance (not to mention patience with this technophobe). My guardian angel, April Olson, for our heavenly lunch dates. Paul Ehni, for the meaningful last weeks with Uncle. My long-time companion and beloved "Bear", John Patterson — without you, every poem would be set in Vancouver!

ABOUT THE AUTHOR

Evelyn Lau is the Vancouver author of fifteen books, including nine previous volumes of poetry. Her first book, *Runaway: Diary of a Street Kid* (HarperCollins, 1989) was published when she was eighteen; it was made into a CBC movie starring Sandra Oh in her first major role. Evelyn's short stories, essays, and novel have been translated into a dozen languages. Her poetry has received the Milton Acorn Award, the Pat Lowther Award, a National Magazine Award and nominations for the BC Book Prize and the Governor-General's Award. Her poems have been chosen for inclusion in both the Best Canadian Poetry and Best American Poetry anthologies. From 2011-2014, Evelyn served as Poet Laureate for the City of Vancouver. Her most recent collection is *Cactus Gardens* (Anvil, 2022), which was included in CBC's Top 20 Poetry Books of 2022, shortlisted for the Vancouver Book Award, and received the Fred Cogswell Award.